Advance Praise for *The Little Book of Big PR*

"Jennefer Witter has walked the walk and talked the talk in the world of PR. Anyone who wants to understand that world better would be well advised to pay attention."

—Julian Epstein, Former Democratic Chief Counsel
In-House during the Clinton Impeachment

"Jennefer's guidance has proven key in helping Luckett & Farley to, as she so often says, gain our unfair share in an über-competitive market. As the founder and CEO of The Boreland Group, Jennefer has been instrumental in providing easy-to-implement tips and strategies to help guide entrepreneurs at any stage to greater levels of success. *The Little Book of Big PR* is required reading for anybody interested in gaining their unfair share, too!"

—Edward Jerdonek, President & CEO, Luckett & Farley Architects, Engineers and Interior Designers

"I have worked with Jennefer since 2006. She knows her stuff when it comes to working with the press. . . . Entrepreneurs would be smart to heed her advice on working with the media."

—Farnoosh Torabi, author of *When She Makes More*; and contributing editor for *Money Magazine*

D1264559

"Heed the solid advice from the consummate PR professional, Jennefer Witter. Her knowledge about PR translates into the results you want. She's helped me and she can certainly help you with this information."

—Barbara Weltman, President of
Big Ideas for Small Business, Inc.

THE LITTLE BOOK
OF BIG PR

The Little Book of Big PR

100+ Quick Tips to Get Your Small Business Noticed

JENNEFER WITTER

AMACOM AMERICAN MANAGEMENT ASSOCIATION
New York • Atlanta • Brussels • Chicago • Mexico City
San Francisco • Shanghai • Tokyo • Toronto • Washington, D.C.

Bulk discounts available. For details visit: www.amacombooks.org/go/specialsales. Or contact special sales: Phone: 800-250-5308 • Email: specialsls@amanet.org • View all the AMACOM titles at: www.amacombooks.org • American Management Association: www.amanet.org

This publication is designed to provide accurate and authoritative information in regard to the subject matter covered. It is sold with the understanding that the publisher is not engaged in rendering legal, accounting, or other professional service. If legal advice or other expert assistance is required, the services of a competent professional person should be sought.

Library of Congress Cataloging-in-Publication Data

Witter, Jennefer.
The little book of big PR : 100+ quick tips to get your small business noticed / Jennefer Witter.
    pages cm
Includes bibliographical references and index.
ISBN 978-0-8144-3621-9 (pbk.) — ISBN-10: 0-8144-3621-8 (pbk.) — ISBN 978-0-8144-3437-6 (ebook) — ISBN-10: 0-8144-3437-1 (ebook) 1. Small business—Public relations. 2. Public relations. I. Title.
HD59.W554 2015
659.2—dc23

2014023984

About AMA
American Management Association (www.amanet.org) is a world leader in talent development, advancing the skills of individuals to drive business success. Our mission is to support the goals of individuals and organizations through a complete range of products and services, including classroom and virtual seminars, webcasts, webinars, podcasts, conferences, corporate and government solutions, business books, and research. AMA's approach to improving performance combines experiential learning—learning through doing—with opportunities for ongoing professional growth at every step of one's career journey.

Printing number
10 9 8 7 6 5 4 3 2 1

To my beloved mother, Freida Boreland, for whom I named my company and who willingly and greatly sacrificed so that I would succeed.

CONTENTS

FOREWORD
by Janet Hanson, Founder, 85 Broads
(now known as Ellevate Network)

It was an easy "yes" when Jennefer asked me if I would consider doing this Foreword. She and I first met through 85 Broads, the global networking organization I founded back in 1997 with the mission of connecting high-achieving professional women with one another. When she mentioned to me that she was writing a book filled with tips to help entrepreneurs use public relations to build their small businesses, I was immediately on board. And I was also excited for Jennefer . . . and for those of you who are about to read her book.

Let me start by saying that I *know* this is a good book. How? By knowing Jennefer and seeing the proof points of what this type of action can bring about. Jennefer has led her successful public relations agency, The Boreland Group, for more than eleven years now. She launched her business as the country was emerging from the shock of 9/11 and the resulting recession and, through her leadership, it continued to thrive through the Great Recession. That says something. And she knows more than just PR—she knows how to run a successful business . . . and not just her own!

Her work has assisted The Boreland Group's clients and helped them get through historically difficult economic times, allowing them to use public relations not just to maintain their businesses, but to *grow* them as well. You'll see that for yourself, as Jennefer, in addition to providing tips, sprinkles in case histories that illustrate how these tactics have been effectively used in real-world business scenarios.

Jennefer's actionable nuts-and-bolts tips are written from the perspective of one small business owner guiding another. They can be immediately implemented into your business model, whether you are a start-up business or an established one. And you will see a difference once you do. The current business environment, while improving, is still challenging; entrepreneurs need every tool they can get their hands on to move ahead. So, take what this book says to heart and start getting, as Jennefer always says, your "unfair share" of business-building attention.

ACKNOWLEDGMENTS

It takes a village to write a book. And my village is populated by many exceptional people. I can't thank them enough for all of their assistance and support. But I'll try:

To the wonderful public relations consultants with whom I work: Elise Blake, Sandy Shen Rice, and Cheryl Sloofman. They are simply the best in the industry.

To all of those who graciously gave their consent and time for the case histories: David Ashen, Tracy Benson, Joan Axelrod, Marc Spector, Scott Spector, and Jacky Teplitzky.

To Janet Hanson for writing a Foreword that far exceeded my expectations.

To Julian Epstein, Ed Jerdonek, Farnoosh Torabi, and Barbara Weltman for providing me with testimonials that were and are truly, deeply appreciated.

To Nathalie Casthely for her great advice and input.

To Ellen Kadin and AMACOM for giving me this opportunity.

To all of The Boreland Group clients. I am fortunate to represent you.

A special thank-you to Filomena Fanelli, who was my right and left arm during this entire adventure, kept me focused and on target, *and* prevented me from walking into oncoming traffic more than once.

Gracias. Mucho.

INTRODUCTION

My goal for *The Little Book of Big PR* is simple: to share the expertise that I have accumulated during my three-decade-plus career in public relations with you, my fellow entrepreneur, regardless of whether you're a veteran business owner or a start-up. There is so much to share, and I wanted to give you as much as possible in order to help you use public relations as an effective, business-building tool.

The genesis of this book came out of the weekly public relations tips that I have been posting on social media over the past couple of years. The response to them from small business owners showed me there is a need for this kind of information. And, I am happy to say, my publisher agreed.

The seven chapters cover the key elements in public relations—the ones I am most frequently asked about. You are getting nuts-and-bolts tips. Here's what I mean: You can take any of these suggestions and immediately implement it into your business model. No lofty theories or 30,000-foot views that sound good and yet leave you asking, "OK, so now where do I go from here?" This book tells you where to go, in the nicest sense. Follow these tips and you will get your "unfair share" of attention. They have worked for me and my clients.

The Little Book of Big PR is a quick read. You can read one chapter and start executing tips or read everything in one sitting and decide which tips will work best for your business now—and maybe later. Sprinkled throughout are "musts" and "must nots," which complement the tip with which they appear. They are simply must-dos in order for the tip to work as well as possible, and cautions against mistakes. I have also included case histories from my files that illustrate, in real-world scenarios, the topic featured in the chapter. I have made this book as user-friendly as possible, and in some chapters, I have included sample content (e.g., a media pitch) for you to use. You can take it straight from the book or modify it as you see fit.

I would love to hear from you. How helpful were these tips? What would you like to learn more about? You can email me at LittleBookofBigPR@theborelandgroup.com and I promise to read every message and respond.

THE LITTLE BOOK
OF BIG PR

CHAPTER 1

Self-Branding

*We are CEOs of our own companies: Me Inc. To be in
business today, our most important job is to be head
marketer for the brand called You.* —Tom Peters[1]

THIS CHAPTER has the longest introduction and the fewest
number of tips, but read it carefully. This chapter is critical, as
it will influence the other chapters in this book: This is why I
selected it to be the first one.

Self-branding is an effective tool to communicate who you
are, what you do, and how you differ from others. This chapter
provides you with the context you need to get the most out of
self-branding. I won't kid you—the self-branding process is a
long one with multiple steps. So, while this chapter only has
four tips, it's the one with the greatest amount of work for
you to do.

Before we dive in, let's define self-branding to ensure we are
on the same page when discussing this tool. The best definition

I have found in my research defines self-branding, or "personal branding" as it is also called, as follows:

> Personal branding is the practice of people marketing themselves and their careers as brands. . . . The personal-branding concept suggests . . . that success comes from self-*packaging*. Personal branding also involves creating an asset by defining an individual's body, clothing, physical appearance and areas of knowledge in a way leading to a uniquely distinguishable, and ideally memorable, impression.[2]

Self-branding is relatively new and is generally considered to have been first identified in a Tom Peters *Fast Company* article written in 1997.[3] I used to work in high-tech PR back in the 1990s, and in that field, the CEOs were strongly identified with their company brands. This was a first, as before then, few C-level executives became the identifying faces for their companies. (Anybody remember the name of the head of Procter and Gamble twenty years ago? Exactly.) Steve Jobs, Bill Gates, Lou Gerstner, Fred Smith: all are immediately identified with their companies—Apple, Microsoft, IBM, FedEx, respectively. I noticed in the early 2000s there was a change, so to speak, in that more C-suite executives built their own brands while they were still within their companies. This is as important for a budding entrepreneur as it is important for an established business owner who wants a strong public association with his or her company, one that complements and furthers the organization, but does not dilute it. Think Sir Richard Branson and Virgin Atlantic.

Self-branding has multiple benefits:

▶ It acts as an identifier as you develop and/or move your business to the next level.

▶ It provides you with a distinct advantage over your competition by highlighting your uniqueness.

▶ It assists in opening doors and building the bottom line.

There are several well-known "self-branders," as I call them, out there who use different elements to highlight their own brands. When you think of Cher, you think of her clothes; Bethenny Frankel, her acerbic wit; Oprah Winfrey, her passion; and Joe Scarborough, his political views. Cher was profiled on CBS *Sunday Morning*, where several minutes were devoted solely to her wardrobe selections and how they defined her. Frankel's verbal quickness made her a standout among the other women on Bravo's *Real Housewives* franchise and eventually led to her own nationally syndicated TV talk show. With Winfrey, you just feel her passion for the projects in which she is completely engaged, from OWN to Lee Daniels' *The Butler*. And Joe Scarborough's small-government conservative principles are the foundation of his popular show on MSNBC, *Morning Joe*.

The following tips will help you to create your own self-brand and make it work for you.

TIP #1 I call it "umbrella-ing." If you're the CEO of your company, you need to create a self-brand that supports your company brand. It can be an element that you own and expand upon. Developing a self-brand that is at odds with your company will cause confusion and lead to mixed messages.

TIP #2 Take the time to *finish* the self-branding process. It will take a while, but do it, because it's worth the time to plan and focus on what you want your brand to be and stand for. FYI: This is the longest tip in the book, as it has several sections to it. Be sure to review each section, as they are inter-related and will have a definite impact on the final results.

There are six steps in the process of self-branding. They are:

1. Define Your Objective. What do you want your brand to accomplish? I usually advise my clients to work backwards. Before you do anything else, define the goal. Then start taking the steps to realize it.

2. Conduct an Audit. You may be surprised at how you see yourself and how others see you. An audit will bring that to the forefront. You need to bridge the gap between reality and perception in order to be successful in creating your self-brand.

For an audit, select between twenty and thirty people to interview. They should be a mix of business associates and clients. Approach them in an email, explaining your request and the purpose of the project. Here's a sample message you can use:

```
Dear (insert name):

I am in the process of conducting an
audit for which there is a dual objec-
tive: learning how I can enhance my serv-
ices to you; and identifying areas for
improvement.

The audit will be a series of brief ques-
tions for which you will have the option
to respond either by email or in a phone
interview. The time you devote to the
audit will not exceed fifteen minutes. I
know you are very busy!

Please let me know by (insert date) how
you would prefer to address the audit and
we'll take it from there.

Thank you in advance for your assistance.
```

A MUST . . . Give your targets the option of emailing responses or doing a telephone interview. People are busy, so providing them with alternatives will be appreciated and may help to increase the number of respondents. Be sure to let them know the entire process will take a short amount of time, as few will want to participate if they think it will be labor-intensive.

Let all targets know that their responses will be anonymous. Have a third party handle the interviews. It can be awkward if you're the one asking the questions and you want your subjects to answer without hesitation and with honesty.

A MUST . . . The person doing the phone interviews must listen, not just take notes. The responses may provoke a question not on the list and unintentionally provide additional information. The interviewer must be proactive in ferreting out as much as possible during the call. The more information received, the better.

My recommendation is to keep the list of questions short. Here are some suggested questions:

▸ What does (name) do? *(This may sound pretty basic to you, but the answers may be revealing.)*

▸ What value does he or she bring to the table?

▸ What can (name) do differently?

▸ What can he or she do better?

▸ List three adjectives to describe (name).

▸ Anything else you would like to add?

You can customize the list with a couple more questions, but limit it to no more than ten.

Once you get all the information, compile the material and review it. What is being said? Are there common threads? What surprises you? Are there areas of opportunity that you need to explore further? I think a good way to review is to list all of the responses to each question in one document. That way, everything is captured in one place and you don't have mounds of paper to sift through. Once the material is compiled, read everything in one sitting. If you need to jot down notes as you read, do it. Let the information sink in. Then read it again. This way, you will become familiar with the material and will catch anything you may have overlooked.

A MUST . . . *You need to be able to accept the findings of your audit. Realize that any criticism you receive is constructive and meant to assist. While the comments may be hard to hear, they will help you grow and strengthen your areas of weakness.*

3. Do Your Research. Go to a search engine like Google and see what is being said or written about you. In addition, look at social media, especially LinkedIn. This is an especially good way to see how others view you. Take a look at your LinkedIn endorsements. Who is endorsing you and for what? In which categories do you get the greatest number of endorsements? Does this match the areas you want to be known for? Or is it an area of opportunity where you can grow? Which category gets the fewest number of endorsements? Are all the categories that apply to you represented, or do you need to add new ones? LinkedIn is a great data-mining tool as you develop your brand.

4. Compile Your Data. Combine the audit results with your research. This is the really hard part: boiling it all down to a self-branding statement that's no more than three, four at the most, sentences. You've heard of the elevator message? It's how you describe yourself or your company in the time it takes to ride in an elevator—about ninety seconds.

This part will take a few attempts
thoughtfully. Aside from "who you are," the
highlight what makes you different and the v
Again, I know this is tough, but with some per
edit it down to the required few sentences.

5. Test It. Once you have your self-branding statement, test it out on a couple of people. Go to a trusted colleague, your mentor, or a business associate and run it past them. You may need to adjust the statement based on the feedback you get, but you won't have to revise the whole thing. The final statement will be the stronger for the external input you receive.

6. Revisit and Refresh. Every year, revisit your statement and see if it needs to be refreshed. It may not, but an annual check will prevent your statement from getting stale. You may need to revisit one of the individuals you asked during the testing phase to see if the statement still works or needs to be updated. Right now, I'm in the process of updating my own self-brand that will further support my company as we move to the next level.

TIP #3 You need to live your self-brand. If you're asked what you do at a networking event, use the statement (but make it conversational, so you don't sound like a robot). If you are doing a media interview, make sure you sprinkle it, as appropriate, into your conversation. Take a look at all your

:n content—whether it's your professional bio, pitch package, or LinkedIn page—and make sure they all align with your statement. You may need to rewrite some content to make sure it is in sync with your branding.

TIP #4 Do you reflect your self-brand statement that you just slaved over to develop? Remember the earlier definition? The Cher example? It's not just about being able to know what you are and being able to verbally communicate it. You need to incorporate image into the mix. Think of Hillary Rodham Clinton and her pantsuits. She fumbled around image-wise until she found her image brand. At first, it was always those black pantsuits. You'll note that she updated her look as time went on. Her outfits, while still the pantsuit template, have a lot more colors, textures, and designs, and she is accessorizing more. And this tip isn't just for women. Charles Osgood, the host for CBS *Sunday Morning,* is known for his bow ties. Tom Wolfe, the celebrated author, is often seen in his sartorial white suits, along with his walking cane—which he doesn't need but is part of his look. And while he is probably too young to be thinking about developing his own self-brand, Dante de Blasio, the teenage son of New York City Mayor Bill de Blasio, is now distinguished for his super-Afro, which received national attention. So, take what you've got or develop a look and use it to your self-brand advantage.

Building Success—
How One Real Estate Broker Did It

Challenge

The value of self-branding became apparent to Jacky Teplitzky when she was featured in a *New York Times* article in 2002. The article spurred such a high level of viable inquiries that Teplitzky decided that she needed to focus on building her self-brand to grow her business and differentiate herself among the thousands of residential real estate agents in Manhattan, one of the most highly competitive housing markets in the country.

Strategy

Teplitzky and her public relations agency defined the areas within her professional portfolio and personal history that would create a sustainable, effective self-brand that would further differentiate her from other agents and support and drive her business goals. Those areas included:

- Her background as a sergeant in the Israeli army.

- Her ability to speak multiple languages.

- Her unusual cultural upbringing: she was born in Chile, raised in Israel, and lived in London and Madrid.

- Her business background and acumen.

‣ Her ability to get transactions done regardless of the degree of difficulty.

Results

Teplitzky's self-branding campaign—along with her willingness to hire consultants to monitor the market and subtly adjust her personal brand as needed—significantly contributed to her growth and protected her during economically difficult times. As of 2003, she had sold fifty million dollars in Manhattan real estate. She worked primarily, at the time, with New York- and U.S.-based sellers, buyers, and investors. By 2013, Teplitzky had sold more than one billion dollars of real estate in Manhattan and Miami, where she had expanded her business. In addition to U.S.-based customers, clients now come in from South America, Europe, and Russia. Despite the Great Recession, she remained a top-producing broker and ranked among elite real estate agents in the country. Thanks to an effective self-branding campaign, Teplitzky's business has thrived, even during the worst of economic times.

CHAPTER 2

Media Relations

Get me on Oprah! —10,000 anonymous clients

OK, SO I'M exaggerating—sorta. When Oprah ended her talk show in 2011, there was an audible sigh of relief among PR professionals worldwide. Not one of us hasn't heard a client say, "Get me on Oprah!"—regardless of her profession or whether or not it was a good fit for her. To be truthful, we all secretly delighted we would never hear that request again.

Getting press is the Holy Grail for many clients. It's the tactic that is most often asked for and it's used as a key measurement for PR companies. In my thirty-plus years in public relations, I have never had a client *not* ask for media relations.

With that said, media relations is not one-size-fits-all. While some entrepreneurs think flashy placements in the *Wall Street Journal* are just what they need, the opposite may be true. There's also a minefield to consider when working with the press (which I will go into shortly). So, let's start talking.

TIP #5 As strange as this may sound, the *Wall Street Journal*—or the *New York Times, USA Today,* or the *Today Show*—may not be the proper venue for you. In selecting press outlets to approach, you need to take a realistic step back. Is this what your industry influencers, customers, or business associates are reading? Is this their primary source of information? While appearing in the *Washington Post* is a major deal, it won't have much of a lasting impact if your decision makers are more heavily influenced by the *Washington Business Journal.* It's not about where you want to be. It's about getting the press that will provide you with the highest returns.

TIP #6 Selecting media outlets is not complicated. The must-haves for most of my clients are industry, consumer, and business outlets. Don't forget that national newspapers also have local sections—the *Wall Street Journal* started the "New York" section a few years ago to great success.

TIP #7 Once you have a list of media outlets, research the reporters who cover your industry. Put together a document that lists their names and contact information so you have everything in one place. This will save time when you're ready to do some pitching. Getting their email addresses shouldn't be difficult. Reporters often include their email addresses in their articles. For broadcast stations, there's usually a page on their websites with contact information. If it's not there, call the outlet. Ask for the editorial department and request the email address of the reporter you want. Sometimes they will give it to you, sometimes they won't. There may also be a general email address where you can send pitches. I avoid those, but if that's all you have to go on, then use it. But try to get the direct address. FYI: Sometimes you get directed to the reporter when asking for an email address. Don't get flustered. Just say, "Hi, I'm (name) from (company). I have a story idea that I wanted to send to you. Can I get your email address?" The reporter may ask you about the idea then and there, so be prepared to verbally pitch your idea if this happens.

TIP #8 A media calendar, also known as an editorial calendar ("ed cal" is a commonly used phrase in industry lingo), is a list of stories that a press outlet intends to write about. Generally, they are issued at the beginning of the year, but the topics are sometimes adjusted throughout the year. They're useful in that they help you see what the outlet is writing about and whether you have a story to pitch to that particular topic.

Most print publications list their media calendars on their websites. While some will have a specific button or section, others will require more searching. If you don't see a specific listing, go to the advertising button and click on it. Sometimes, the ed cal will be there. Other times, you may need to click on and search the media kit option.

In print, you have long- and short-lead publications. The former means that they will start accepting editorial inquiries three to four months ahead of the actual publication date. For example, they'll start collecting leads in March for June stories. Short-lead can mean that the turnaround time is as short as one day—or less—so you have to act fast. Short-leads usually don't have editorial calendars to support them, so it's catch-as-catch-can.

TIP #9 This is such a big MUST that it deserves its own tip. I'm sorry to say that the biggest beef that reporters have with PR professionals is that they get a lot of pitches that don't apply to their areas of coverage (also known as their "beats"). They get really cranky about that. Keep in mind that reporters get *a lot* of emails. I've heard from some that they get as many as 300 messages a day, sometimes more. They need to go through each one, so getting information that doesn't apply to them is a major time drain, and it eats up a lot of their band-width. If the person sending the message doesn't know basic information—what the reporter writes about—why should the reporter pay any attention to this pitch or to future pitches?

Therefore, it is critical for entrepreneurs to spend time learning reporters' beats. Go to their LinkedIn pages and read up. Follow their tweets. Go to the media outlet's website or Google them by their names, and a list of stories will pop up. Go back at least six months, and you'll see a distinct pattern to a reporter's writing style and story selection. Once you determine you have the right person, then it's time to pitch.

TIP #10 What is a pitch? A pitch is a brief note—two or three short paragraphs at the most—outlining the story angle and why it is of interest to the reporter. Whether you're pitching yourself or your company, you need to highlight your expertise on the topic. Include speaking engagements where you have addressed the topic or white papers that you've written on the subject.

If you have already been featured in a news story, include a link to the piece. It provides third-party credibility. *Don't* send a clip from a competitor's outlet. You won't get coverage. You can send trade coverage to a consumer publication or even to another trade magazine if it covers a different market section. And include the line, "I can go into more detail about this topic," to show there is more to cover and that you're not going to rehash already-reported news.

The subject line should read: "Story Concept." Let the reporter know right off the bat why you're contacting her. Keep the fluff talk out of it. Get to the point. For example, "Dear (reporter's name), I wanted to touch base with you regarding a story concept that I believe is of interest to your readers (or audience, if you're pitching broadcast)." Then go into the pitch. End on a note of action: "I'll contact you once you've had the opportunity to review this information." Don't wait for her to call you.

If the reporter has already covered the story and you have an opposing or a fresh viewpoint, then your message should read: "Dear (name), This is in regards to your article (insert title) that appeared on (insert date). While I found it of interest, I wanted to offer a differing viewpoint." Then, go into it. The action end-line should be, "I would be more than happy to go into greater detail. I'll contact you shortly to determine your interest."

Always say thank-you. "Many thanks for your consideration" should be the last line of every pitch. And include your company name, a link to the website, or your LinkedIn profile so the reporter can easily research you. Those should be included in your signature.

TIP #11 Try not to include attachments in your pitch. There are a lot of bugs and viruses out there, and reporters hesitate to open attachments from an unverified source. As much as possible, embed the information in the body of the email.

TIP #12 Once you send the pitch, wait a couple of days before contacting the reporter again. If you're nervous about calling her, send a follow-up email. Resend the original email with a note that says, "I am following up on the below. Please let me know if you're interested in the story. Again, many thanks for your time." If you don't hear back, then move on. Multiple emails or calls will irritate reporters. If they are interested, they'll get back to you.

If you do choose to call, keep it brief. This is important: Know when their deadlines are. It all depends on the publication date for print media. If it's a weekly that comes out on Mondays, avoid calling on Thursdays and Fridays. Dailies? Don't contact them after 2:00 P.M. Print reporters usually start around 10:00 A.M., so calling in the morning may be your best time. Broadcast? It depends on their airtime. I would not reach out a couple of hours before airtime. Reporters on deadline can be quite nasty when they get interrupted.

When you call, say who you are, note that you sent a pitch and when, summarize it, and ask if there's interest. Don't babble. And don't take it personally if they say, "No," and hang up. It happens—not often, but it does. Most of the time, they will listen and reply. If they're not interested, say, "Okay, thanks for your time." Don't try to persuade them otherwise or argue with them if they don't want to proceed. That's a surefire way for them *not* to take your future calls.

TIP #13 Here's a *big* no. Don't send the same pitch to more than one reporter at the same outlet at the same time. I was at a seminar where an editor of a major news daily said he and his colleagues would sometimes get the same exact pitch sent to them from the same person. As he said, "We all share information, so we know when we get the same thing." Find one reporter and pitch that person. Pitching multiple reporters will not increase your chances of getting a placement. It will only make you look like you don't know what you're doing and lessen the chances of you being taken seriously by the outlet. Don't do it!

TIP #14 Another big no relates to exclusives. An exclusive is when you give a media outlet the right to be the first to publish your story. The press loves to get a first crack. The benefit to you is that you know you will be getting coverage in your outlet of choice.

There are a couple of methods: You can promise an outlet a specific exclusive (e.g., only to *Good Morning, America*), or you can give multiple exclusives, usually only to one broadcast outlet and one print medium, which will appear on the same day. For the former, you need to be very specific: "I am offering this to the *Chicago Tribune* as a newspaper exclusive." Or, if you're doing multiples, "I am offering the newspaper exclusive to the *Chicago Tribune* and the broadcast exclusive to CNN." This way, both outlets are fully informed from the get-go who is also being included in your outreach. Send separate emails to each outlet. Don't group them.

A MUST . . . Honor your agreements! If you get an exclusive, you cannot have anything appear before the agreed-upon date of publication. That will break the exclusive agreement. Once the story runs, you can issue the press release to the general press.

T**IP #15** There are different broadcast interview types:

▸ Live: The interview is being broadcast in real time. You can fall, trip, or forget what you want to say. The cameras will keep rolling.

▸ Live-to-Tape: This is when the interview is taped in real time. A lot of evening newscasts follow this format. While it is not live, the taping will proceed without pause.

▸ Taped: This is my preferred mode for my clients. Here, if you stutter, spill coffee, or whatever, it can be edited out of the final version. It's a more comfortable environment and less nerve-wracking for the individual.

You can't ask broadcast outlets for taped interviews. You have to go with what they have, meaning that you need to be prepared . . . which leads us to our next tip.

TIP #16 If a reporter calls you, respond as quickly as possible. I have had clients miss out on opportunities because they took too long to respond. If you don't have the time to do an interview, let the reporter know. She or he will appreciate it.

TIP #17 If you pitch a story, be sure you can discuss it in detail. Sounds like a no-brainer, but it isn't. I had a client who proposed a great story concept, which I pitched to an influential national news organization that liked the idea. However, when the article came out, my client wasn't quoted. As it turned out, he only had superficial knowledge of the topic and his interview responses were weak. If you don't know, don't pitch.

TIP #18 "No comment" is a gray area. This usually happens in times of crisis. By saying "no comment," you run the risk of the story being developed without your point of view. However, you may be advised by your attorney not to comment. If that's the case, take the advice.

TIP #19 If you're asked a question that you can't answer, do not wing it. Say, "I don't know. Let me get back to you." If it's a live broadcast, say, "I'm not familiar with that . . ." and segue to a point you can discuss in detail.

TIP #20 Media training is extremely useful, especially if you have never been interviewed. A good trainer will walk you through several different scenarios to help you prepare for interviews. When I worked at Ketchum, a global public relations firm, they had an entire department devoted to media training. The firm even built a mini-studio to recreate the feeling of an actual television set. It was of great assistance to our clients.

My best advice is to hire a professional trainer to work with you directly. Check the PR industry trades and get references. It's a worthwhile investment to make, especially if you or your company is in a sensitive situation.

TIP #21 If you're being interviewed, it's okay to have a cheat sheet. A cheat sheet outlines key points that you want to make. Keep it to one page. Don't be surprised if you get nervous; I've been interviewed multiple times and I still get nervous. Having a cheat sheet acts like a security blanket. You may not get to all the points, but at least you won't forget any. And once you get going, you probably won't need it.

It's easier to use a cheat sheet in a radio interview. You can refer to it and no one will see you looking down. On TV, use an index card. Briefly review it just before you go on air. You can glance down once or twice during the actual interview, but that's it. You don't want to look unprepared. Remember, it acts as a backup, not as a primary source.

> **A MUST NOT . . .** *If you're being interviewed for the radio,* don't read from the cheat sheet. *It will make you sound stilted and unnatural. You know your stuff; otherwise, you wouldn't be interviewed. Only refer to the document as a refresher or if your mind truly goes blank.*

TIP #22 At the end of the interview, if you haven't been asked about what you consider to be an important point, say, "I would like to add . . ." and launch into the point. Reporters will appreciate the effort, and the information can open up another avenue of questions. On time-limited interviews, such as television and radio, you will need to make the point fast—like in five seconds. Otherwise, you'll be cut off.

TIP #23 The nuances of speaking "on the record," "off the record," or "on background" are tricky, even for people with lots of experience in doing interviews. Don't take the risk of releasing information that can come back to haunt you. Assume a reporter will publish everything you say. The best rule is this: If you don't want the reporter to write it, don't say it.

TIP #24 Developing a relationship with reporters is vital. They will come to trust you for your opinion and see you as a reliable resource, whether it's for interviews or acting as a sounding board for potential story ideas. That relationship is developed over time and depends on your being available as much as you can be for the reporter. I have had the good fortune of having many wonderful relationships with reporters. Aside from appreciating the fact that I know their beats and what to pitch, they know I will go out of my way to help them. There have been times when they were looking for sources that are not covered by my accounts, but if I can connect them with the right people, I do it. I respond promptly to their requests. And I honor exclusives. My clients have greatly benefited from these relationships, and a happy client is a happy Jennefer.

TIP #25 Once your placement appears, don't assume that your network has seen it. Distribute the hit to your targets via e-blasts. Post on social media. Or highlight it in your newsletter or in a marketing letter. And don't forget your staff—your most important audience. They need to know when and where the placements occur, how they can use them, and why they are important.

When distributing to your network, you must avoid appearing overly boastful. Here is suggested wording for an e-blast or post:

```
I am so pleased to be included in this
(name media outlet) article (insert
title). In the piece, I discuss (topic).
I hope you find it of value. And please
know I would be more than happy to dis-
cuss it with you in greater detail.
```

TIP #26 Sometimes, you do an interview and your quote doesn't appear. It can happen for a number of reasons:

▶ The reporter decided to go in a different direction.

▶ They conducted too many interviews and can't fit all the interviewees in the article.

▶ Your quote was included in the manuscript but was edited out in the final version.

▶ Due to space constraints, your quote was deleted.

All of the above has happened to me. What you need to do is follow up with the reporter to find out why you weren't included. If the case was that your answers weren't usable, find out why. That will help you with the next interview. And if it's one of the reasons stated, don't get all snarky with the reporter. Be gracious and say, "Regardless of how it turned out, thanks for reaching out to me. I appreciate it." A lot of times the reporter will get back in touch with you with another article. But if you are rude, well, the reporter may just skip over you—permanently.

TIP #27 If you appear on television, here are some things to consider:

> Avoid white. It's hard to shoot and the color has a tendency to bleed. Busy prints, such as plaids, are also difficult to shoot. If you wear a white shirt, cut it with a colored scarf (if you're a woman) or a solid-colored tie and jacket (if you're a man).

> Find out beforehand if they are going to do your makeup at the studio. If not, go to a cosmetic counter—my go-to is MAC Cosmetics—and tell the makeup artist that you're going to be on television. They'll apply appropriate makeup. For free. And, yes, this goes for men, too.

> If you're sitting, ladies, cross your legs at the ankles. Cross at the thighs and your dress can ride up and your thighs appear fatter. And who wants either?

▸ Ladies, if there is one item of makeup you *cannot* overlook, it has to be false eyelashes. They'll make your eyes pop and avoid a washed-out look. Trust me on this.

CASE STUDY •

Media Relations as a Business-Building Tactic

Challenge

Scott Spector, AIA and principal at Spector Group, a leading New York–based international architecture, master planning, and design firm, had a specific demand regarding traditional media: He wanted to reach a business, rather than a trade, audience. The business community was his primary target, and getting into the media outlets that they read and respected would further differentiate his company from other architecture firms. It would allow him to reach these decision makers via influential and trusted third-party vehicles.

Strategy

A media list was created with an emphasis on local and national media, along with an editorial calendar, which focused on appropriate articles. Story pitching was done with business angles, which were brainstormed between Spector and his PR agency, and one-on-one meetings were arranged with media outlets such as *Dow Jones*, the *Wall Street Journal*, and *Crain's New York*

Business so that Spector could introduce the company and proactively come up with story ideas with the editors.

Results

Spector has been consistently featured in a plethora of business media, ranging from *Dow Jones* and the *New York Times* to MarketWatch Radio Network and *Investor's Business Daily*. He has also appeared in the Associated Press, *TheStreet.com*, and the *New York Post*. Spector has used these placements in both new business development and as a recruitment tool. As his visibility and expertise became more widely known, the *Commercial Observer*, a must-read publication for New York City–based commercial real estate decision makers, approached him to do a weekly online column. He agreed and is now the only architect to present his views on a myriad of industry topics and positions directly to his primary client base. His articles are among the better read and followed, according to the *Observer*.

CHAPTER 3

Social Media

Social media is here. It's not going away; not a passing fad.
Be where your customers are: in social media. —Lori Ruff[1]

HERE ARE THE three reasons I always hear from entrepreneurs as to why they are not using social media:

1. "I'm too busy."

2. "I'm a private person."

3. "They're for dating, not for business."

Let me address each of those complaints:

Too busy? My fellow business owner, we're *all* too busy. But as an entrepreneur, are you too busy to build your business? Of course not. You can spend as little as thirty minutes a day on social media and still see dramatic results. I spend that, on average, and have accomplished a lot, including:

▶ Generating actual revenue.

▶ Booking interviews with major media.

▶ Networking.

▶ Writing this book.

A private person? So am I. But for my business, I get as public as possible. If my targets don't know anything about my company, how am I going to build my business? And if my competition is out there, all over social media, my absence is not golden—it shows that I am not using all available channels to communicate effectively with the groups of people who influence and affect my business. After all, you're not being asked to list your weight and Social Security number. You post what is specifically relevant to your company.

Just for dating? At the beginning, yes, Facebook was a social site in the truest sense of the word. And, yes, many still use it to talk about their personal lives. But Facebook is a now a tool that businesses use to communicate directly to their audiences—and it's time you jumped aboard. Look at how many big businesses have active Facebook pages: Kraft Foods, IBM, Ford Motor Company. Do you think they would waste their time with this if it didn't add to the bottom line—the goal of every business, regardless of its size? LinkedIn has always been a business site, and I have many friends and colleagues who are active on the site and have generated business and gotten job offers.

Every entrepreneur should be using social media. Here's why:

- Your audience is online. According to Nielsen's 2012 Social Media Report: "Consumers around the world are using social media to learn about other consumers' experiences, find more information about brands, products and services, and to find deals and purchase incentives."[2]

- When used properly, social media can build and extend your brand, generate revenue, introduce you to new audiences, build relationships with existing audiences, act as networking tools, and allow you to control your message.

- If you are not on social media, you can bet your competition is—and building their market share at your expense.

With all that said, I need to underscore the fact that social media is not a magic wand. You won't start practicing it and see results overnight. And it, alone, cannot advance your business. It needs to be a component of your entire business plan in order for it to work. Here are some tips to help make that happen.

TIP #28   The first thing you need to do is decide what your objective is in using social media. Is it to build brand reputation, recruit employees, attract new audiences? Once you decide what your goal is, you need to decide which social media tool to use.

There's an abundance of social media tools out there, and they are constantly changing. Keeping up with them and using them can become a full-time job. But you don't need to do that. I truly believe you need to pick and choose which social media will provide a return on your investment in an effective and efficient manner. With that in mind, I am going to focus on Facebook and LinkedIn. These are among the oldest of the social media tools out there, and they offer proven results for businesses. Pinterest is all the rage, but I don't see it being widely used by the business community. And while Twitter is always notable for big events, such as elections or celebrity news, I don't view it as providing the same consistent results for entrepreneurs as Facebook and LinkedIn do.

TIP #29   If your audience is primarily business-to-business, then LinkedIn is your tool. If it's a mix—business and consumer—you can use LinkedIn and Facebook. If you strictly want to focus on consumers, use Facebook. It will take time to build a presence and start to see feedback, regardless of the tools you use.

T**IP #30** What makes a good Facebook page? One that consistently offers fresh and interesting content. You can make your page a go-to site by including information of interest to your audience, such as news articles, industry events, and the like. Post company updates like major new hires or milestones. Keeping your Facebook friends involved and informed will attract positive attention and build your profile with your target audience.

T**IP #31** To keep your Facebook friends reading and commenting, you need to post on a regular basis. Some sites post a dozen or more times a day on Facebook. That's too much. Some post once a week. Too little. For Facebook, post at least four times a week on different days. Images and short videos increase engagement. In addition to posting the kind of content I've suggested in the previous tip, here's another recommendation: post quotations. For some reason, people just love reading quotes. I notice a lot of quotes from motivational speakers like Tony Robbins, historical figures such as Winston Churchill, and even biblical quotes. Just know your audience and understand that whatever quote you choose has to be relevant to their interests.

You can also find out what your audience is thinking by asking open-ended questions. For example, if you're a financial planner, an open-ended question could be:

"My biggest financial worry is _____." You can leave it up to your Facebook friends to respond.

Or, if you want to grow specific areas of your business and aren't sure on which area to concentrate, then you can shape the question accordingly. For example:

"My biggest financial worry is _____

    a) saving for retirement.

    b) saving for my kids' college tuition.

    c) managing my aging parents' financial assets."

You can then shape posts to address the most popular items. And you can contact individuals directly, based on their responses, and offer them personal consulting.

A MUST . . . The following strategy has worked wonders in building my brand and expanding my company's visibility. What is it? Posting a "Tip of the Week." People love to learn and get "inside" information that can assist them. Obviously, don't share proprietary information. My "Tip of the Week," which I posted on social media, was the genesis of this book. The attention I received showed there was a genuine interest in the material, and I shared that fact with the publisher, who agreed.

TIP #32 Ideally, your Facebook page should contain some personal information, perhaps one or two posts every other week. Including some non-work postings will show you as a well-rounded, interesting person, not some work automaton. But don't show a picture of yourself drinking straight from a beer keg—and, yes, I saw that on a business page. Instead, mention volunteer work or what your book club is reading.

TIP #33 If one of your friends is recognized, say for an award, share it on your Facebook page. It shows selflessness, and the person will appreciate it. In return, she may share information of yours on her page, thereby expanding your information to a fresh set of friends and potential clients.

TIP #34 Should you create a Facebook business page for your company or an individual business page? A business page focuses solely on the company, such as new projects, corporate milestones, personnel, industry news, and the like. An individual business page highlights the *person's* business activities, such as seminar presentations, awards, etc. It also features select personal information that provides a fuller, more "human" picture of the person. Which one you choose to create is up to you and the objective that you've set for yourself. What will relate the best to your target audiences? Once you decide that, then you can create the page.

TIP #35 Can you have both a professional page that showcases you, the individual, and one for your company? Yes. I've seen it done many times. Define the goals for each and the audiences you want to attract for each page. Some targets may carry over to both pages, so while you can repeat some content, you also need to create original posts for each page.

TIP #36 Both Facebook and LinkedIn are great virtual networking tools. You can stay in front of your targets without ever leaving your desk. For Facebook, comment on and/or "like" other people's posts. This way, you remain visible in a subtle, nonintrusive manner. And here's a bonus: By showing up on their page, most times your targets will visit your page and see what you're doing. Facebook news feeds carry a fraction of what your friends are posting, so don't take it for granted that every post will be seen. Or read.

And yet another benefit: When you're ready for a face-to-face meeting with someone you've established a relationship with on your social media, you won't go in cold since you've already laid a foundation from which to proceed.

> **A MUST NOT . . .** Don't "like" or comment solely to get in front of the person—she'll see through you in a minute. Be authentic and the rest will take care of itself.

TIP #37 Now, let's address LinkedIn. LinkedIn is much more formal than Facebook, which I see as being more like a conversation with your friends. LinkedIn is more businesslike. And since you only get to use 200 characters, you need to be brief. A well-written business summary and profile are important. Have a photo, preferably one that is professionally taken. Studies show that having a picture increases your chances of being viewed. References should be up to date—nothing from five years back.

Should you do a professional page or a company page on LinkedIn? I say have both. They are complementary, and, as an executive, you have more information to post on your page than on a company page, which is more broad-based. Company pages should, of course, include a company summary, the products offered, key executives, company updates, awards, media mentions, and the like. Professional pages have a company summary and your responsibilities at the firm, but the primary focus is on you, the individual. Posts can include information such as speaking engagements or honors. The page should also include endorsements, a relatively new feature on LinkedIn where the user can select the skills he wants to have endorsed and his connections endorse him on the ones they select. It's a great third-party tool to demonstrate your expertise and knowledge.

T**IP #38** I also encourage you to join LinkedIn professional groups. This is an area that many overlook. It's a great way to see what is being discussed in your industry, and it's also an opportunity for you to showcase your expertise by starting or commenting on discussions.

T**IP #39** I feel the number of postings on LinkedIn is pretty fluid. I do think that you should post content at least twice a week. That should complement the discussions you participate in and/or start. You don't need to participate in every group every day, but post at least once a week per group to keep your presence known.

On a related note, don't "overgroup," that is, don't join groups simply to join groups. It's quality, not quantity, that matters here.

T**IP #40** When you connect with someone, always check out the groups she belongs to. They may be of interest to you or beneficial to your company.

T**IP #41** Don't just join industry-specific groups. I advise my clients to look at vertical groups. For example, for my women executive clients, I suggest they look at groups such as ForbesWoman—and for my client CEOs, I suggest CEO or

C-suite groups. Here, you can exchange ideas and information, and perhaps even create meaningful relationships.

T|IP #42 When you join a group, be sure to read their regulations regarding posting, content, etc. Many do not allow self-promotion or solicitation. Some rules are pretty strict. If you violate them, you can get kicked out.

T|IP #43 Your entire LinkedIn page should be updated at least once a year. Change your picture, freshen up your bio, add new skills, if appropriate. This shouldn't take a lot of time. Some of the content can be tweaked or just a few sentences added to refresh the copy.

T|IP #44 You can start your own LinkedIn group. It's easy to set up. The majority of time will be spent administering the group. Some groups allow for open posting while others review all posts before they are allowed to appear online. See what works best for you and how much time you can spend on it. A group that goes dead doesn't reflect well on you.

T|IP #45 If you get a Facebook friend request or LinkedIn request and you don't know the person or share a professional connection, don't accept the request. You won't hurt their feelings if you don't connect with them. They won't stalk you. Most likely, they will go away quietly.

A MUST NOT . . . Do not post your year of birth in your birthday date. That is a gold mine for identity thieves. Don't post personal information on someone else's wall—about yourself or about the other person. A friend of mine asked on my wall about a date I had. I immediately took it down and asked her to send me all such questions via private email. And don't sell your wares on other people's pages without their okay. This happened to me when a business associate posted on my page information about his recently published book. I took it down and sent him a note that he was never to do that again without my permission. Don't irk your network or take it for granted. The loss may be greater than you think.

TIP #46 You can tie your posts together on LinkedIn and Facebook, using a variety of easily available tools. HootSuite is one where you post once and it travels across a variety of platforms. Personally, I don't like it. The point of social media is to create conversations and build virtual relationships. A sterile post that goes out to all channels lacks customization. A friend of mine posts her tweets on her Facebook page, and she gets very little feedback. You may want to try it for yourself, however, and if you're not pleased with the results, go back to individual postings.

TIP #47 LinkedIn and Facebook are *great* data-gathering and analysis tools. On Facebook, you can see what is trending in real time via the news feed function and use that information to your benefit. For LinkedIn, see what people are endorsing you for. It shows how they perceive you. If the perception does not match your reality, it's time for a review, both of your page and of your self-branding. Or, you may see an opportunity to expand into an area that you previously had overlooked.

TIP #48 If you really don't have time to do the posts yourself, have someone in your company do them. Do not use an intern or any other temporary worker who doesn't know your company. Sit with the person weekly to go over that week's proposed posts. Determine what to post, when, and where. The person should also have the power to post in your name on other pages, but make sure she checks with you before doing so—always.

TIP #49 There's a lot of back-and-forth about the best times to post. Some say weekends are good for Facebook, while others say to avoid posting on Saturdays and Sundays. For LinkedIn, the best times are usually just before or after work—never between 9:00 A.M. and 5:00 P.M. Play around and see what works best for you.

TIP #50 Don't get into fights in social media. I've seen this happen when a person disagrees about a post. Most of the time, it gets messy and very few people win. If you feel strongly about a post and think you can comment in a cordial manner without name-calling or throwing insults (yes, I've seen that more than once), then go forward. But understand the risks and anticipate the consequences. It's probably best if you send a private message with your complaint.

TIP #51 As with polite conversation, stay away from controversial posts on social media. Religion, politics, abortion—you know what to avoid. I had a Facebook friend who posted a series of vitriolic posts, using derogatory, distasteful, and disrespectful language, during the 2012 presidential election. She got a lot of nasty comments. Was it worth it? No. Did she gain anything from it? No. Did it advance her business? No. Does she wish she never did it? I don't know—I defriended her.

TIP #52 This last tip is probably the most important in this chapter. The online world is unforgiving. What you say and do online tends to stay there forever, even if you delete it. And more corporations are checking the Facebook and LinkedIn posts of current and future employees. It's not illegal to fire someone—or not hire them—because of a post.

Businesses you may want to partner with are eyeing those pages as well. If they don't like what they see, they may not connect with you. So, think twice before you post. And if you're not sure, don't do it. The consequences aren't worth it.

CASE STUDY • • • • • • • • • • • • • • • • • • •
Food for Thought
Challenge
Love & Quiches Gourmet®, one of the nation's leading dessert and quiche manufacturers, engaged my firm, The Boreland Group, to create a comprehensive public relations program, of which social media would be a critical element. Though they had a social media presence, they were not fully utilizing the medium as a business- and brand-building tool.

Strategy
To meet the company's stated objectives, we developed a detailed plan to leverage their social media presence. Our tactics included:

> ▸ Holding weekly meetings with the company's president and executive vice president to discuss events and activities in which they were engaged—and helping them determine which social media were the best for communicating the information.

- Creating and executing a Facebook contest designed to increase "likes," hence expanding its brand and knowledge of the company's popular products to new audiences. Prizes included cheesecakes, quiches, and brownies. Information was posted on a variety of pages, and to participate, all one had to do was "like" the page. The contest was open to existing fans, as well, to keep them engaged. A cause-related marketing element was added to make the contest more meaningful: For each new "like," one dollar was donated to a nonprofit committed to the fight against childhood hunger, a cause Love & Quiches Gourmet has supported for a long time.

- Launching a series of branded posts to complement the company's fortieth anniversary campaign.

- Posting articles in which the company was featured to further the awareness and reach of such placements to the company's target audiences.

- Advising the company to follow, comment, and engage on other food pages and industry groups on both LinkedIn and Facebook—pages and groups that supported the brand and acted as virtual channels to communicate the latest news.

Results

Since the inception of the social media campaign, Love & Quiches Gourmet has seen a 40 percent increase in its Facebook "likes" and an excellent response to its LinkedIn activity. "I have received many appointment and project requests through LinkedIn," says Joan Axelrod, an executive vice president at the company. "It's a very useful complement to my in-person outreach."

CHAPTER 4

Networking

*Networking is an essential part of building
wealth.* —Armstrong Williams[1]

I HAVE A secret. I didn't start actively networking until I
started my business in 2003. I have always said that if I had
networked like this when I first started working in the early
1980s, I would be Queen of the World by now.

Networking is a critical component of business success.
The business environment has changed since I started The
Boreland Group eleven years ago—and much more so since
the Great Recession. Before 2007, when a handful of companies may have gone after the same piece of business, now
scores of them are, meaning we all have to work longer and
harder, and in some instances we do so for the same, or even
a lesser, amount of revenue. In other words, it's a dog-eat-dog

world, and the dogs we are talking about are Rottweilers, not the fluffy ones with the pink bow clip-ons.

Networking is a tool that opens and gets you through the door. You'll have a stronger shot at getting additional business if you put into practice a smart networking strategy. And, as with everything, you need to evaluate the results: If you're not getting a return on investment, then it's time to examine your methods and start anew.

Now, start networking and boost your returns with the following tips.

TIP #53 I've found that many people feel about networking as they do about public speaking. In other words, they would rather have a root canal than head into a room filled with strangers. I sometimes feel that way myself. I once got this tip: "Go to the person who scares you the most and introduce yourself." It has helped me tremendously in making the first move. You'll find that person is not so scary and is probably even relieved that someone is speaking to her. A simple, "How did you hear of this event?" works. You can work your way into a circle and say, "Hi, I'm new here. My name is . . . Yours?" They'll work you in, and if not, find another group. Keep in mind that it's never personal. And if they don't want to talk with you, then you don't need to talk to them.

TIP #54 You could network five times a day, every day, if you wanted to. But we're business owners, and we have other responsibilities to address during our workdays. What you have to do is be network-smart. The first thing to do is to figure out what your objective is, whether it's to source out a business opportunity, build your brand, or investigate a new field. Once you determine your goal, do some research. What are the influential groups that can help you the most? Note, I said "influential": It's not size that matters—it's quality and the ability to connect with people who will help you achieve your goal. Ask around, go to a couple of meetings (most groups have non-member nights), and talk to members directly. If you find a small group, that's fine. All you need to make a difference is that one connection.

TIP #55 How do you select a networking group? Go to the groups where your targets are. Several of my clients are in real estate, so I have served on the board of directors of the African-American Real Estate Professionals of Washington, D.C. The connections I have made there—and the friendships that I have formed—are priceless. Think outside the box. Join a group that has nothing to do with your work. One of my clients belongs to an influential organization that has nothing to do with her craft. She joined because of her deep commitment to its mission. She became involved in the organization, volunteering her time, fundraising, speaking on panels, etc. She made a difference. And of course you know what I'm going to say next. She got viable business leads from those in the group who got to know and trust her (and also because she's great at what she does). So, do some creative thinking and go with one less-than-obvious group.

TIP #56 To make the most of my networking experiences, I set three goals for myself before I step foot into the room. For example: meet a new person; find out who is in charge of the speaking engagements; and find a person who may be a good strategic partner. Your goals, of course, may be different. What's important is having specific goals; it sets a context around the experience. Once I achieve those goals, I decide whether to stay or go. I usually stay, since I am so comfortable by then, it's nice to continue the conversations and meet new people.

TIP #57 While I belong to several networking groups, I am selective about which ones I join.

A MUST . . . You need to know how many hours you can devote to networking. If it's one hour a week, then I suggest you limit yourself to one group. Again, it's all about quality, not quantity.

And here's the next question: Is that hour best for you in the mornings, evenings, or on the weekends? If the group you belong to always meets first thing in the morning, and you have a standing senior staff meeting every day at 8:00 A.M., that's not going to work. The groups I belong to have various meeting times that fit with my schedule. My suggestion is to plan against your standing meetings the time you have available. And, yes, there will always be an emergency that precludes you from attending an event or a meeting. Some groups have a requirement on how many meetings you can miss. Find out what it is and keep track of the times when you miss a meeting.

TIP #58 Learn what is required of you before you join a networking group. There's a national business networking group that has chapters across the country and thousands of members. For the chapter in my town, members meet over breakfast and exchange business leads. Only one person per industry is allowed in each group, so if you're in advertising, then you'll be the only person in advertising within your group. The group requires that you regularly provide leads to other members. I attended a meeting as a guest and found the members to be extremely professional and supportive. It's a wonderful organization, and members have benefited greatly. But it wasn't for me—the pressure to dig up leads outside of my own work was a burden I did not want to carry. And the break-of-dawn breakfast meetings took place in a restaurant that was about an hour's commute from my office. So, with these factors in mind, I declined the opportunity to join. Again, this is a fruitful organization for thousands of professionals, just not for me.

TIP #59 Dropping out of networking groups is not a crime. Networking takes time, energy, and effort. You will not see the fruits of your labor right away. I belonged to a women's real estate group and was a member for about three years. I went to their events, met some great women, and made some strong connections. But no business came out of it. I decided to leave it, and while attending one of my very last lunches, I sat next to a woman whom I had never met. Turns out her company was looking for a PR company. She took my card and arranged a meeting with the CEO. In a matter of weeks, I signed a new account—and one that brought in enough money with that first check to cover my first three years in the group. The point is, you need to invest the time, explore all opportunities, and be active. But if nothing comes out of your efforts, and you have truly done as much as you can, then leave.

TIP #60 When you join a group, you need to be proactive. Don't expect opportunities to plop into your lap. Find out if they have committees that you can join. If you can, host events at your workplace. If there are opportunities for sponsorship, shell out the money. And, most of all, talk to people who are there. I went to a networking event and actively worked the room. I mentioned that I give presentations and before I knew it, I was offered the opportunity from one of the attendees to be a co-presenter at an already-planned speaking engagement. I accepted, as the audience was one of my key targets. Don't be a wallflower. Do not meld into the background. Remember, networking can lead to revenue, but you need to work at it to get it.

TIP #61 Now, networking is not all about me—or rather you. It can't be. As I tell my clients, you must be able to give, as well as graciously receive. Always, always ask what you can do for others—"How can I help *you*?"—even if there's no immediate benefit to you. Those who are perceived solely as takers will not get much in return. Networking is truly fifty-fifty. If you can't give, then stay in the office.

TIP #62 Never leave home without your business cards. You never know who you'll meet! I take my cards with me everywhere—to the hair salon, manicurist, grocery shopping. I always keep a few in my wallet in addition to my card-holder. (If you're a woman, you know that switching purses means something is invariably left out.) Because many times when I have left the house without a business card, I meet someone who should get it. So, along with your keys and smart phone, carry those business cards.

TIP #63 Virtual networking is an underused tool. You can network 24/7 from your laptop, mobile device, or desktop. As you know from the previous chapter, you should be active on Facebook and/or LinkedIn and like or comment on posts.

> **A MUST . . .** *You need to be authentic in your social media. If you're doing so simply to be visible, your postings will come across as fake or phony— and that's the kiss of death. By networking virtually, you develop a relationship with your targets. And when you're ready to reach out, it won't be out of the blue, as you have already been consistently in front of the person.*

TIP #64 Don't let networking contacts go cold. You can meet dozens of new people every time you attend a networking event. In order to stand out from the crowd and maintain the momentum you've begun to generate, make sure to follow up with a note within at least five business days after meeting a new person. This will help fuel the process of converting the person from a casual acquaintance to a new client. It can also lead to referrals.

TIP #65 I'm often asked how to stay in contact after the initial note is sent without seeming like a stalker. Easy. Keep a database of those people you want to stay in contact with and "touch them" at least once a month. Of course, I don't mean go out and tackle them. The "touch" can be as simple as sending an article that you've read and think they would be interested in knowing about. If they have won an award or reached a company milestone, send a congratulatory note. If they're going to a tradeshow that you're also attending, suggest meeting up at the event. One of the things I do is invite contacts to my speaking engagements. I either get comp tickets or pay for the tickets myself. For the latter, it's worth the investment, and the gesture is always appreciated. I went to a presentation where the head of the organization said that she always tries to do something "nice" once a week for someone in her networking circle, without any expectation that the gesture will be returned. For me, "nice" is making an introduction or sharing a lead I heard about that may assist them. Whatever the "nice" is, it is always noticed and remembered.

TIP #66 When you're at a networking event, don't whip out your business card as soon as you're introduced. Too crass and totally off-putting. Talk a little about what you do, hear from the other person, and when appropriate, exchange cards: "By the way, here's my card. May I get yours?"

TIP #67 You're speaking with someone and it turns out to be a dud contact—yes, that happens and you know it does—cut it short and move on. But don't be rude. End the conversation with, "It was so nice to have spoken with you. Thanks for sharing your time with me." And find the next person to talk to.

TIP #68 Talking with strangers sometimes leads to awkward pauses in the conversation. For some reason, people can't stand a few moments of silence. But whatever you do, don't fill the void by bringing up controversial issues. Starting off a conversation with, "So, what do you think about those drone strikes?" won't do—trust me. It can be something as routine as, "This weather is crazy, isn't it?" And if the pause lasts, it's a signal to gracefully end the conversation and start a new one with another person.

TIP #69 I recently went to a networking event and saw two people chatting. Well, one was talking while the other person scanned the room. Not nice. When someone is speaking with you, whether it's a good or bad contact, give him the courtesy of your attention. And, as I said above, you can gracefully end the conversation without looking like a boor.

TIP #70 A networking contact leads to direct business. Congratulations! Now, do you need to reward that person? You can certainly take the person out to lunch, donate to his favorite charity in his name, or send a thank-you gift (for example, a gift certificate). Acknowledgment is a good business practice and something many of us forget to do.

TIP #71 There will be times when you and a key competitor are in the same networking group. Obviously, you're going after the same business. But you shouldn't take flight and leave all those potential leads to your competition. Explore your options by talking to the group's leaders and seeking out ways to differentiate yourself. A smart strategy will allow you to maximize your presence within the group. For example, if your competitor is sponsoring a golf outing, you might consider hosting an awards dinner or some other high-profile event that will resonate with the group while distinguishing you from the competition.

TIP #72 The best networking group can be the one you create on your own. I've seen a proliferation of networkers starting their own groups on social media, especially on LinkedIn. Creating your own group gives you immense latitude: you invite the people you want to grow your connections with; there isn't direct competition since you obviously won't be inviting your rivals to join; and there's flexibility to the theme.

With all that said, it does take effort to create a successful group. Investigate the more successful ones in your circles and adapt their best practices, as appropriate. Consider having a virtual *and* physical group: that is, have the group live on LinkedIn but include physical meetings as well. I've seen a rise in those. Put together a plan: how many times you want to meet; where; what void it will fill; whom you are inviting; what the group's theme will be; and so on. Think of a catchy name. Just keep in mind that the measurement of success is how much time you are willing to put into the effort—in return for what reward.

CASE STUDY •

Networking + Authenticity = Business

Challenge

Networking is a well-known way to build business, but for Tracy Benson, founder and CEO of On the Same Page, a business consultancy firm, doing so in a way that felt "authentic and organic," rather than strategic and self-serving, was paramount. All relationship-building activities needed to fit with the openness of the company's culture—and the way that the firm interacts with its clients—for them to be effective.

Strategy

On the Same Page built its professional network through a number of activities, including:

▸ Being active members of industry associations and taking leadership roles, as appropriate. For instance, two of its team members have served as presidents of the board of the Communication Leadership Exchange, and others have served on committees or are active in the Public Relations Society of America (PRSA) and the International Association of Business Communicators (IABC). This allows them to meet and work with people they might not have otherwise become involved with; and it allows others to experience, in a hands-on way, what it's like to work with On the Same Page and its team members.

▸ Cross-pollinating within parallel industry organizations and attending events, where applicable. For example, one team member has a Ph.D. in industrial psychology and belongs to the Society for Industrial and Organizational Psychology (SIOP). Each year, he attends SIOP's annual conference. In recent years, other members of the On the Same Page team have accompanied him. They have found the experience to be a valuable way to meet new contacts, increase their knowledge, and improve their skills, enhancing their value to clients.

‣ Creating community by hosting informal networking functions in the various cities they work in. Several On the Same Page executives host monthly breakfasts, lunch gatherings, or dinner get-togethers to stay in touch with peers and share ideas and synergies.

‣ Proactively staying in touch with contacts, providing relevant information and research that applies to them, either personally or professionally, and building friendships in the process.

Results

On the Same Page traces approximately 80 percent of its work projects back to relationships formed through networking, proving that when connections are made genuinely, results come naturally.

CHAPTER 5

Speaking Engagements

There are only two types of speakers in the world. 1. The nervous and 2. Liars. — Mark Twain[1]

I ENJOY public speaking. "Well, good for you, Jennefer," you're probably thinking. There is a natural fear of doing a presentation (see this chapter's very first tip). But if you're an entrepreneur, bite the bullet and do it. Public speaking is an excellent tool to get in front of your target market, showcase your expertise, and differentiate yourself and your company from the competition. You can generate new business or receive business leads or referrals. One of my clients, a realtor, got a multimillion-dollar listing that resulted from a speaking engagement. That should motivate you!

The following tips will help you approach public speaking with a little less trepidation and assist you in getting the most out of your efforts.

TIP #73 Does the thought of speaking in public give you the heebie-jeebies? You're in good company. According to the National Institute of Mental Health (NIMH), 74 percent of people have a fear of public speaking.[2] There's even a term for it: glossophobia. My advice to you, dear entrepreneur, is: Get over it, and fast!

Everyone is nervous before she speaks, and if people tell you otherwise, they're not being truthful. I'm a Nervous Nellie, too: I conjure up ways of getting out of the engagement ("If I fall down and twist my ankle . . ."), my heart races, I think I'm going to forget everything. These are common feelings. But you gotta do it anyhow! What should calm you down is that you know your stuff—you weren't selected as a speaker as a favor to your mother. Because you are respected, people want to hear what you have to say. No one is going to throw tomatoes at you if you seem a little anxious at the start. The attendees want you to succeed because they want to learn from you. Take baby steps at first by starting with small groups. Focus on one presentation topic instead of several, so you get really comfortable presenting, and then move up to larger groups and grow your subject list. Take it slowly. Just the fact that you are doing this already separates you from most in your field. And you may even grow to like presenting. Really!

TIP #74 Another common fear is that no one will show up—which would be really embarrassing! That's why you need to actively promote your presentation via traditional and social media, word-of-mouth, and in conjunction with the presenting venue. I helped to launch one of my client's ventures into public speaking. For her first presentation at an extremely prestigious venue, she and I developed an aggressive strategy to ensure a large audience. My firm created content for a series of e-blasts that she forwarded to her database on a timed schedule. We produced a press release and calendar listing and mailed them to trade and consumer media. We also invited the media, highlighting the topic and its relevance to their respective audiences. In addition to developing her bio and sending a photo of the client for inclusion in their brochure, we kept the venue informed of all our activities. The results: a packed house. A local cable television station covered it, and several reporters, including one from a national news outlet, attended.

The first step for you is to promote your presentation. Here's content for a sample e-blast to your database:

```
I'm very pleased to be presenting at
(insert name of venue), where I will dis-
cuss (insert topic) on (insert date). If
you're interested in attending, please
click here for registration information
(insert link). I hope to see you there!
```

Remember to test the link to be certain it works before sending it out.

Next, find out how the presenting organization is promoting your speech. If it's a press release, ask for a copy of it to send to your database (it can be a follow-up to the first blast you do). If an article results, send that out as well, because it provides additional credibility. Here's sample content for an e-blast if you get an article placement:

> (Name of publication) just ran an article (or calendar listing) on my (insert topic name) presentation at (insert name of venue). I am so excited about the coverage and, of course, the opportunity to present. Here's the piece (insert article or calendar listing link). Hope you can attend!

Regarding a timetable, one blast every other week is fine. One week before the event, send out two, and the day before, send a final blast. Suggested content:

> Tomorrow is the big day! I am so looking forward to my presentation (insert name of presentation) at (insert venue name) on (insert day and time). There are still a few seats left, so if you haven't had a chance to purchase a ticket, there's still time. Hope to see you there!

Confirm, of course, that tickets are still available.

TIP #75 The media can be an important part of your presentation. Ask the presenting organization if they're inviting press. If not, consider sending an invitation to your media list (see Chapter 2). However, first confirm that you are allowed to invite the press because some venues don't allow it. Here's sample copy for a press invitation:

```
Hi (name):

I am presenting on (insert name of topic)
at the (insert name of venue) on (insert
date/time). I would like to extend an
invitation to you to attend as my guest.
I feel your audience will be interested
in the subject. Of course, I am available
beforehand if you would like to speak
before the actual event. I'll touch base
with you shortly for your response.
```

I always like to end with the "I'll be in touch with you . . ." line rather than "I look forward to hearing from you." You have greater control this way, and it gives you a reason to follow up.

Be aware that while some media outlets pay for their tickets, others do not. Be prepared to pay for the tickets yourself.

Once the press is there, pay attention to them. Reserve seats for them in the front, so they don't go searching for seating—

and they have a good view of you. Make sure the venue has their names on a list (if they are being comped), so they can enter the location without a hassle. Provide your cell number in case they need to reach you. And you *must* send a thank-you note the next day.

Will this guarantee coverage? No. But it will further your relationship with the reporter, and that can translate into coverage at a later date.

TIP #76 You may want to consider buying and giving away tickets as a strategic tool to build attendance: business or professional acquaintances, and especially key clients. It's a nice gesture. You may also buy tickets for company employees who want to attend and support you—or, if you'd prefer, chip in and contribute 50 percent of the cost. You can also ask the venue if they provide comp tickets and, if they do, distribute accordingly. Yes, it's all an investment, but it will pay off.

TIP #77 Offer attendee incentives: a gift certificate; a donation in the person's name to his or her favorite charity; or, if you're feeling generous, raffle off an electronic device, such as an iPad or iPod. There's a dual purpose here: In addition to generating attendance, you can gather data by collecting business cards for the drawing.

Have the drawings or giveaways at the end of your presentation. And make sure the winner has to be in attendance to receive the gift. While your presentation will undoubtedly be scintillating, it's further encouragement for attendees to stay until the end.

> *A MUST . . .* Whether you have three or thirty people who show up, you must give your all to the group, out of respect for those in attendance. One of those thirty—or one of those three—may come through for you in a big way. It only takes one person to make a difference.

TIP #78 Where should you speak? There are obvious venues, such as tradeshows, networking groups, and the like. But don't overlook other locations that can be of value. Public libraries are great places to present. I have presented at the Science, Industry and Business Library in New York with great success. Find out if your children's schools offer opportunities for parents to present. One of my clients, a realtor, presented at her son's public school after clearing it with the school's administrators. Why? She works with a lot of families and she shared information on the local housing market that was pertinent to them. Academia is also another target—many colleges and universities have entrepreneurship programs. You can share your knowledge with the next generation of small business owners while personally scoping out fresh talent whom you may want to recruit. You can investigate presenting at the local YMCA or YMHA, or even to your building. As for the latter, I found out that many of my neighbors are small business owners. You guessed it! I am working with the building's management company to do a presentation. Whatever you consider, make sure the audience is one you want to target. Don't present just to say you've presented. To present to those who have no interest in your topic is a waste of time.

TIP #79 Rehearsing is a critical component of a presentation's success. I rehearse three or more times before the actual presentation. But that's me: I'm pretty anal. The bottom line is you need to rehearse *more than once*. You owe your audience a quality presentation, and that includes rehearsing your stuff so you offer a smooth and informative session. Nothing less is acceptable.

If you want, rehearse before a couple of people. Their feedback will be helpful, and it will probably make you more comfortable when you do your actual presentation.

> **A MUST . . .** *Do at least one rehearsal standing up. Believe me, it makes a difference from doing it sitting at your desk. Many presentations are done on your feet, not sitting down.*

TIP #80 Keep the audience engaged. While you'll probably have a Q&A session at the end of your presentation, ask the audience for their interaction. I usually say, "I want this session to be interactive. There'll be a formal Q&A, but feel free to ask a quick question or two during the presentation. And if I'm unclear, let me know and I'll clarify the point." Attendees pay greater attention and appreciate the opportunity to participate.

Another way to engage is to ask the audience a question during the presentation. It will act as a mini-jolt and encourage them to pay closer attention.

Finally, if you're a solo presenter, step out from behind the podium and walk among the audience. I did a presentation at The Power Conference, an annual business development conference for professional women in the Washington, D.C., area. I left the podium and walked among the attendees for a portion of the presentation. It's a wonderful tactic to connect more closely with the audience.

TIP #81 There are many types of speaking engagements— workshops, panels, webinars, etc. At the Power Conference that I just mentioned, they had workshops and roundtables. The former were for larger groups and took place in rooms, without strict attendance limitations; the latter took place at actual round tables and were limited to ten participants.

Decide what works best for you and your topic. If you're not sure, contact the education coordinator, and she will provide you with direction.

TIP #82 You need to determine what you need in terms of audiovisual (AV). Those who like to walk around prefer clip-on mics. Some, like me, prefer hand-held mics that can be attached to the podium or removed, allowing for mobility. I like options. Get to your location early to test-run the presentation, because you'll have enough pressure on you already. A technical glitch just before you start adds enormous stress and can throw you off your game. Always have backup (the anal in me, again). If you have a PowerPoint presentation, and for some reason your laptop goes haywire, you'll still have paper notes to go by. Have the presentation saved both on your laptop and on a memory stick. As the Boy Scouts recommend: "Be Prepared"—because something always goes wrong.

TIP #83 What if you're asked a question that you can't answer during the Q&A session? Don't fake it. Be upfront and say that you'll need to research the question and get back to the audience member with an answer. Making up a response that turns out to be wrong can and will damage your reputation. Honesty is the best policy.

TIP #84 What tools should you use to communicate with your audience? It all depends. If the group prefers Power-Point, gussy it up a bit with graphics and movement. The bells and whistles will help to keep their attention. If they prefer a conversational style, use index cards. Just keep in mind that nothing replaces good, hard, informative substance. Weak content in a pretty presentation is like a pig in a Tory Burch outfit—it's still a pig.

TIP #85 There's a pretty clear line between presenting information and doing a blatant commercial for your services. The latter is a big *no*, and you will not be invited back if you do so. You are there to educate and inform—not to shill for your firm. I once invited a reporter for a major newspaper to present at a client's seminar. She talked about the paper's advertising, which was *not* the topic that we discussed before-hand. The audience got really annoyed, and my client was peeved. The reporter wasn't invited back. You can subtly work in a mention of your company by using it once or twice to illustrate a point. The reference should be quick, and then you move on. Otherwise, it will have the smell of a sell, and you can lose more than you gain if that happens.

TIP #86 It's always disconcerting when people walk out during your presentation. It happens! Don't freak out—

keep going. If you see the person or persons afterwards, ask graciously by saying, "I saw you leave earlier. Do you mind telling me why? Your feedback would be really appreciated." This can be a bit uncomfortable, but it should be a learning experience.

TIP #87 Do you want to be a moderator or a panelist? There are benefits to both. The moderator is akin to an orchestra conductor—she has full control of the speakers and is the lead. The panelists have more speaking time and can really showcase their expertise. I've had clients turn down opportunities to be moderators because they felt being a panelist had more value. Figure out what works best for you.

TIP #88 If you want to do a solo presentation but get a request to be on a panel, take it. Don't let ego get in your way. Being part of a select group of recognized professionals is an honor, and your industry standing will be elevated as a result.

TIP #89 Creating a seminar on your own is a lot of work but can be one of the best things you do. Why? You have control over the content, can select the venue, and can decide whom to invite, either as attendees or guest speakers. But keep in mind that planning a seminar takes months. Here's a quick checklist for you:

▸ *What's your budget?* Once you decide on the budget, you can plan accordingly. Most speakers do so for free. Add in a stipend for travel costs or meals if you want to and can afford it.

▸ *Decide on the topics.* Trends are always of interest. Take a look at underreported subjects. Test out the selected topic on a group of industry colleagues and see if there's interest.

▸ *Decide when to hold the event.* You should look at dates that don't conflict with major events or local industry activities. Masterplanneronline.com is an event site that lists events that are happening in several major markets. You can also check trade magazines, which usually list upcoming events.

▸ *Select the venue.* Can you hold it at your business location or at an event space? How many people do you expect? Is it centrally located? From firsthand experience, I've learned that in Washington, D.C., planning events near a Metro stop boosts attendance. The same is probably true in other large cities. Have you considered holding an event in your building? I have an apartment in Bethesda, Maryland, located near a Metro stop and several large parking garages. I held a seminar in the business lounge, which holds thirty, has a great AV system—and was available to me at no cost.

▸ *Are you serving refreshments?* At the building where I held my seminar, I served supermarket-bought pastries. And they were gobbled up. You don't need to spend a lot to keep people happy.

‣ *What time of the day?* Some people prefer Saturday conferences—no work pressure and more flexibility in their time. Poll your target audience and see what the majority prefers.

‣ *Are there guest speakers?* Are you going to be a solo presenter or are you inviting guest speakers? How many? What are they going to cover? How will they complement each other? Are they required to bring in guests? If so, how many?

‣ *Will there be panelists?* If you are having panelists, have at least one conference call before the meeting to go over the agenda and their respective roles. This call will ensure that everyone is on the same page.

‣ *Thanking your guests.* If you have guests, consider thank-you gifts—a bottle of wine, flowers, a fruit basket, something to show your appreciation. Plus, *always* send a thank-you note.

TIP #90 It's never too early to investigate speaking opportunities at tradeshows. Many slots book a year in advance. So make a list of the shows where you want to speak and find out—ASAP—their deadlines for RFPs (Request for Presentations).

TIP #91 This is a personal pet peeve of mine. Too many women hesitate to give presentations. I once organized a panel and asked three women, all accomplished professionals, to participate. And all of them turned me down—because they were *too nervous*. I was able to lure one in by saying I would sit next to her (I was speaking, as well). The two men accepted immediately. Ladies, get over your fears. We can give birth, fly to the moon, and run countries: speaking in front of a group should be easy-peasy.

TIP #92 I always ask for speaker evaluations. They're invaluable sources of information. You need to know what struck a chord in the audience and what left them cold. That type of information will strengthen your next presentation and make you a more professional presenter.

TIP #93 Find out if you can use the information from the evaluations as testimonials. Ask the conference manager. These are great third-party testaments to your ability, and they attract additional attention. If you are given the okay, post on social media, use in other presentation applications, share with your staff. You have to walk a fine line between sharing and boasting. Suggested content for general posting:

```
I had a great time at (name of confer-
ence) where I presented on (name of
```

topic). And I'm happy to note that others had a great time as well, judging from the feedback I received.

(insert no more than two quick comments)

I appreciate the opportunity to speak on (topic) and am really honored that (name of conference) gave me the chance to do so. My deepest appreciation to them and to those who attended my presentation. Thank you, again!

TIP #94 How do you keep the interest going once the presentation is over and collect valuable data at the same time? Promise to email copies of your presentation. It's a great way to collect email addresses to add to your database.

TIP #95 Don't go crazy once you have the email addresses. There's nothing worse than getting spammed. Be selective about what you send. Company newsletters, upcoming speaking engagements, and commentary on industry issues are good places to start. Send out once a month. That gentle touching base will be just enough to stay in front of them without becoming an annoyance. And knowing that they are getting interesting material will encourage recipients to open your emails. However, do include an option for them to opt out. It's the polite thing to do.

Enhancing Your Professional Stature

Challenge

Marc Spector, AIA, NCARB, and a principal at Spector Group, a New York–based international architecture, master planning, and design firm (see the case study in Chapter 2), wanted to complement his already established visibility within the architecture community. He had previously leveraged speaking opportunities as part of his public relations program with us at The Boreland Group, presenting on topics ranging from "Real Estate Repositioning: A Strategy for the New Economy" to "Green Retrofitting of Public and Private Buildings."

Strategy

TBG investigated influential engagements outside of the usual opportunities for architects. The platforms had to support the overarching objective for Spector—to reach a wider circle of contacts and differentiate his business from competitors. With that in mind, among the forums TBG approached were the 92nd Street Y and Yeshiva University's Sy Syms School of Business. The former is one of the most prestigious venues—and one of the most difficult in which to get placed—in New York City, attracting speakers such as Bill Clinton, Tony Blair, Elie Wiesel, and Frank Gehry. The latter is one of the nation's leading business schools, with a highly selective policy for speakers. Past presenters have included Mickey Drexler (CEO and chairman of the board,

J. Crew), Michael Bloomberg (the former mayor of New York City), and Sumner Redstone (chairman, National Amusements).

Results

For the 92nd Street Y, TBG proposed a presentation featuring a one-on-one conversation with Spector and a writer who had previously interviewed him about Arne Jacobsen, one of the most influential architects of the twentieth century and a role model for many of today's architects. Spector would discuss Jacobsen's career, his lasting impact on the design community, and his influence on Spector's own design sensibilities. The 92nd Street Y accepted the proposal, and Spector presented to an enthusiastic and receptive audience.

TBG approached Yeshiva University's Sy Syms School of Business for Spector to present as part of the school's Doris and Dr. Ira Kukin Entrepreneurial and Executive Lecture Series. The pitch was that he would discuss his company's growth tactics, including their expansion overseas. He would also address working within a family business and transitioning the business from father to sons. Yeshiva accepted the concept, and Spector became a member of an elite group of speakers to present at the school.

Meeting Spector's stated objective, the nontraditional engagements broadened the firm's reach, introduced the company to new audiences, and widened his sphere of influence in a strategic, thoughtful manner.

CHAPTER 6

Cause-Related Marketing

Do well by doing good. —attributed to Benjamin Franklin

CAUSE-RELATED marketing (CRM) is dear to my heart. Also known as "cause marketing" and "corporate social responsibility," CRM is when a for-profit company aligns itself with a nonprofit or a cause and proactively supports it.

Aside from doing good, corporations can receive significant benefits to their own business by engaging in CRM. According to a Nielsen 2013 "Consumers Who Care" study, 50 percent of global consumers said they "would be willing to reward companies that give back to society by paying more for their goods and services[1]. . . ."

However, CRM can backfire if it's perceived that a company is engaging in cause marketing solely to build business, with no true commitment to the cause. The following tips will walk you through the process and help to ensure a positive outcome for all involved.

TIP #96 The key to a successful cause-related marketing campaign is being authentic. You must select a cause that you truly care about—not one based solely on the anticipated dividend. If your commitment is not genuine, you can damage your standing with the cause, your target audiences, your staff, and your business.

TIP #97 Before selecting a cause, determine what your objective is and work from there. Do you want to attract a new audience? Do you want to build deeper relationships with your existing targets? Do you want to differentiate yourself from your competition? Think about what you want to achieve, and that will help narrow down the selection process.

TIP #98 Involve your staff during the selection process. It's important for them to understand what you're doing and why you're doing it. They may want to participate, which is all the better for you. The more the merrier!

A MUST . . . I've worked at companies where the staff was practically force-marched into participating in the firm's CRM program. Some of my colleagues went along grudgingly—they either didn't support the cause, had their own charities they supported, or were simply not interested. They went along because they feared that not participating would damage their standing at the company. If you want your staff to be involved, make it voluntary. The ones who want to participate will step up. And the ones who don't shouldn't be made to feel guilty. They may change their minds after they see the program in action.

TIP #99 It's important to be realistic about how much and what you can commit to. There's nothing worse than promising the moon and later realizing that you're in over your head. No matter how well intentioned you are, you still have to run a business. How, exactly, will you help? Will it just be you? Or will the staff be included? How much time will you be able to give? What about budget? Will you be making annual donations, sponsoring activities, or donating a percentage of earnings? Answering some of these basic questions early will be of great assistance as you move forward.

TIP #100 You can engage in a successful CRM program even if you are a small business with limited financial resources. There are many things you can do that don't involve a direct cost. During the holidays, there's a plethora of activities from which you can choose, whether it's helping out with a coat drive or collecting toys. You can make the effort an annual event to further underscore your commitment and association with the group.

TIP #101 Once you have identified a cause, contact the executive director of the organization and arrange a meeting. Treat it like an interview. Find out what they need. Who are their other CRM partners? What are they looking for in terms of time? Financial commitment?

There's also an important nontangible to consider. While you're not looking for a friendship, a good working relationship is critical to the success of the partnership. If there's a personality clash, it's best to investigate another charity.

TIP #102 We all know the saying "Date before you marry." The same thing goes for CRM. Once you select the cause, do a test-run before you publicly announce the relationship. See how well you work with each other. Give it a couple of months before you formally commit. If it's a one-off, such as a coat drive, do it one year and see how it works out. If it works, then make a formal announcement the next year. If the relationship doesn't work, have a backup cause that you can connect with.

TIP #103 While giving back is good, you're preneur, and you're doing this with the ex it will benefit your business. Subtly leverage ment. Begin by discussing with the organization how they will communicate your involvement. Will it be announced in a press release or featured in their newsletter? Do they post on their social network information about the work they do with corporate partners? Will it be highlighted on their website? Most causes have a system in place to publicize their CRM relationships. Find out what your nonprofit's system is and take advantage of it.

On your end, there are several things you can do, such as:

‣ Highlight your participation in your email signature— "(Your company name) is a proud supporter of (name of nonprofit)." Hyperlink to the organization to underscore the relationship.

‣ Post your partnership with the cause on your home page, using the same language as in your email signature.

‣ Announce the relationship in your company newsletter, and be sure to explain why you are supporting the cause and what kind of assistance you are providing. Feature regular updates—say, once a quarter—on the organization and/or on your support. (Updates don't necessarily have to be focused on your company. They can be on the milestones the cause

...elf is accomplishing, bringing into greater focus why you selected them and the good work that they do.)

▶ Post monthly updates on your social media. If the non-profit has a Facebook page (and it probably does), be sure to comment and/or like their posts (but remember, post authentically, not just to get your name seen).

TIP #104 You need to measure your results. Are you achieving your objective? If not, revisit the program and make necessary adjustments. It does take time—months, and sometimes years—for results to occur. However, to make sure you are going in the right direction, conduct annual reviews to see where you are, what needs to be tweaked, and how well you are working with the group. Patience is required. That's why being authentic and truly committed to the cause is important.

CASE STUDY • • • • • • • • • • • • • • • • • •

Love Fights Hunger

Challenge

Love & Quiches Gourmet® has long been passionately involved in the fight against hunger, and CRM has always been an important component in their business model. As such, when they hired a public relations agency, they wanted to showcase their CRM activities. The goal was threefold: to further raise awareness of their long-term and passionate efforts to support the causes they felt strongly about; to utilize CRM as an opportunity to further differentiate themselves from their competitors; and to show other small businesses that it is possible to contribute to a cause, just as many larger corporations with bigger budgets and more resources do.

Strategy

Love & Quiches Gourmet devised a CRM strategy that was actively and thoughtfully implemented. The company:

▸ Used social media to raise awareness of the company's ongoing efforts to battle childhood hunger, including creating and launching a Facebook contest where a dollar was donated to a nonprofit committed to the fight against childhood hunger for each new "like" Love & Quiches Gourmet received.

▸ Posted photos and updates on Facebook and LinkedIn when the company and/or staff participated in charitable events or donated goods to the favored causes, always including a focus on the cause itself.

▸ Secured key media placements to allow the company to talk about its giving and the reasoning behind it. A highlight was a more-than-four-minute interview on MarketWatch Radio Network, in which Joan Axelrod, the company's executive vice president, educated and informed companies on the intricacies of CRM, its benefits, and pitfalls to avoid.

▸ Widely distributed a press release highlighting the donation that Love & Quiches Gourmet made to Island Harvest, Long Island's largest hunger relief organization, a nonprofit with which the company has built a successful relationship. The release included quotes from the charity, along with information on how the contributions were able to assist the group. A photo of a check presentation was included and featured executives from the receiving organization and the Love & Quiches Gourmet staff.

Results

Love & Quiches Gourmet successfully showcased its CRM program in a nonboastful manner while continuing to build on its long-standing reputation as a company that truly cares about its community. It has subtly differentiated itself from its competition and has shown its generosity to others in the business community by being open about how to run a successful cause-related marketing campaign.

CHAPTER 7

Selecting a PR Agency

*If I was down to the last dollar of my marketing budget,
I'd spend it on PR!* — Bill Gates[1]

THANKS, BILL. I'm here whenever you're ready to spend that dollar!

Many turn to a public relations agency or a consultant when they want to receive the full benefits of the discipline but don't have the time or expertise to practice it themselves. Whether it's for a long-term relationship or a one-off project, here's what you need to consider after deciding to outsource the PR function.

TIP #105 One of the first questions I ask when I'm approached is, "What's your budget?" Once I find out, I know whether to move forward or suggest they use a consultant. A full-service agency is more costly than an independent professional. There's no harm or detriment in working with a consultant. You will still get quality work but at a price you can afford.

TIP #106 Looking for a public relations agency or consultant but don't know where to begin? There are many PR firms and consultants to choose from. Talk to business associates, relevant trade associations, and even reporters who cover your industry to get recommendations.

TIP #107 I always suggest an in-person meeting as part of the selection process because chemistry is so important. PR is frequently listed as one of the most stressful careers to have. And it is. I think it's important that the client and I have mutual respect and, yes, a liking for each other. A dysfunctional or adversarial relationship will definitely negatively impact the account—and add to the stress levels of both parties.

TIP #108 When interviewing a PR firm or consultant, ask them to discuss their background and show the results of their efforts, such as media placements or booked speaking opportunities. Some may use case histories to showcase their work, and that's fine. Ask them how they would approach your account. Ask for a proposal, which is a road map that outlines how they will promote your business. At the bare minimum, it should include objectives, strategies, and tactics. Costs must be included. Based on the meeting and the plan, you should be able to determine whom to choose.

A MUST NOT . . . If you decide not to select a PR agency or consultant after all, you can't use any of the ideas that were presented. It's their intellectual capital, and implementing their concepts without their approval or an agreed-upon remuneration is unethical.

TIP #109 New clients are often surprised at their level of involvement in the early stages of their relationship with a PR agency or consultant. The agency is learning your business and setting up the account, all of which takes time. Your involvement will lessen as the account matures.

A MUST . . . A successful partnership between you and your PR partner requires participation from both. The agency or consultant must consistently be proactive, while the client must respond as promptly as possible. If either neglects his or her responsibility in the relationship, the relationship will suffer.

TIP #110 Be direct with your PR partner. If they do something you don't like, tell them. Keeping it to yourself just allows the problem to fester. They won't know that there's an issue—much less what the issue is—if you don't tell them. And they could make the same mistake again, unknowingly. Arrange a sit-down or a telemeeting and nip the problem in the bud.

TIP #111 I always say this: It is my job to provide a recommendation to the client and it's up to them to accept it—or not. My goal is for my client to make a fully informed decision based on my expertise. If they choose not to go along with a recommendation, I'm fine with that, but I wouldn't be if I felt that they were making a decision without having explored all aspects.

TIP #112 A PR agency or a consultant, while your partner, is not your friend. It's not their job to rubber-stamp any and all of your ideas. In my career, I have had to push back hard when I felt the client was going in the wrong direction. It's not comfortable, but a solid relationship will survive the disagreement.

TIP #113 One of the biggest mistakes a company can make after they hire a PR agency or consultant is to withhold important information. When this happens it is usually because of a lack of understanding about how to work together to maximize the relationship. To that end, before you launch the relationship, commit to the idea of a partnership and know that information-sharing is part of the process. The more your PR partner knows about your business, the more they can help you.

TIP #114 This sometimes happens: A public relations agency or consultant will announce a great success and then be surprised when the client doesn't share their enthusiasm. Make sure that you and your PR partner share the same definitions of success before any work commences. That definition should be included in the PR proposal. While PR can be nebulous, there are certain tactics against which measurement can be placed. For example, for media interviews, the program should note how many should be accomplished within the program's timeframe. That way, you have a hard number to work against.

TIP #115 Have realistic expectations for PR. I once had a client for whom we lined up interviews with the *Wall Street Journal*, Bloomberg News, and a trade publication within the first two weeks of the relationship. And they were unhappy, feeling that we were not doing enough. I eventually resigned the account, as it became clear they would never be pleased with the results my firm was producing on their behalf.

TIP #116 And speaking of terminating an account, you should have an exit strategy with your agency or consultant in case it comes to that. In my contracts, I include a two- or four-week option, depending on the length of the agreement, for clients to opt out of the relationship. Mind you, it has never happened. But if it were to happen, my firm would have the opportunity to wind down the account, produce a summary report, and ensure that as many loose ends are tied up as possible. Leaving with grace and dignity is the best way to go. But it shouldn't come to that. As mentioned earlier, if you have any issues, address them right away; but should they continue, well, it may be time to cut your losses and move on.

TIP #117 How long should a contract last? I feel that retainer contracts should last at least six months. When starting a program, you have basics to address—like creating a media list, developing an editorial calendar, creating a positioning statement—and all that takes time. Anything shorter than six months and you may be shortchanging the process.

TIP #118 There are retainer accounts and project-based accounts. The former are long term and ongoing and usually cover a wide range of tactics, from speaking engagements to social media to cause-related marketing. The latter are finite—with a defined beginning, middle, and end—and focus on one tactic or project. Project-based accounts are usually less expensive than retainer accounts. You can still do several projects a year, but you should plan out what needs to be done, because if you need multiple projects, it may be cheaper for you to do a retainer account.

TIP #119 Some clients ask to pay on a placement basis. In other words, they'll pay once the interview is printed or aired. I never accept those terms; it just doesn't work. There is a lot of work that goes into pitching, securing, and arranging interviews. And just because you are interviewed doesn't automatically mean that your quotes will be included. I once worked a full year on what was to be a major feature with the chief executive officer of my client company, a global technology firm, in an influential business magazine. Then 9/11 occurred, my client's market category collapsed, and the story was no longer deemed relevant. The whole thing was ditched.

Usually, quotes get cut for less dramatic reasons—most often for space restrictions or because the writer goes in another direction—all of which are out of the control of the

PR professional. If a potential client insists on a program with payment based on placements, that's fine with me. I won't be working with them, though.

TIP #120 Be crystal clear when discussing expenses: what will and won't be covered under the agreement. You may want to put a cap on individual charges: for example, insisting that anything over $200 has to receive written approval. Outlining what is to be expected will avoid sticker shock when you get the bill.

TIP #121 If you think that public relations alone will boost your revenue, you need to know it won't happen. The PR component has to be part of an overall, comprehensive business plan where all the strategies and tactics are in line to produce an expected outcome. I always ask to see a prospect's business plan to ensure that the program I write will support and help achieve the goals of the organization.

CASE STUDY • • • • • • • • • • • • • • • • • •
Decisions, Decisions
Challenge
David Ashen, principal and founder of dash design, a leading interior design and brand consulting firm specializing in hospitality and retail projects, understood the benefits of engaging

a public relations agency. The firm had previously worked with a consultant—and had also tried going it solo—and noticed a measurable increase in visibility when it had a professional leading the charge.

Though they had retained an agency and had achieved a regular presence in design industry publications, dash design wanted to widen its focus to include mainstream business media and commercial trade publications widely read by the C-level decision-makers with whom they wanted to be "top of mind." Doing so would build brand awareness of their growing firm and showcase its niche expertise and noteworthy client roster and projects to a broader audience.

dash design sought out a new public relations agency—one that could look at the company with a fresh perspective and take an innovative approach. To ensure the search process went smoothly, the firm laid out the specifics of what they wanted in an agency:

- The ability to raise the group's visibility using a variety of public relations tools including media relations, speaking opportunities, and social media.

- Familiarity with the design industry.

- Existing relationships with local, national, and international business media; radio and television contacts; and hotel, restaurant, and retail publications.

> ▸ The capacity to work independently and proactively to develop creative story ideas, media outreach, and speaking engagement opportunities.

> ▸ A history of achieving measurable results.

Strategy

dash selected my firm, The Boreland Group (TBG). We met all of their qualifying criteria. In addition, Ashen had become aware of TBG's work through the recommendation of a journalist and by witnessing our continued successes and long-term relationship with one of its existing clients. In meetings and discussions with TBG's CEO (moi!), Ashen was impressed by the extensive research and preparation that went into the company's public relations plan and the detailed questions I asked before laying out tactics, deliverables, and a timeline to achieve them. The approach was exactly the kind of out-of-the-box thinking dash design was looking for.

Results

The results were more than satisfying for Ashen. "We strongly feel that TBG's critical business thinking and strategic approach brought value to the table and helped us highlight the quality and scope of our work among new audiences," says Ashen. "Our public relations program hit all of the objectives outlined and even exceeded them. We consider the partnership to be a great success and one that will aid us as we continue to grow as a company."

Among the highlights within the first six months of the program, we:

▸ Secured a total of thirteen placements for the firm, more than had been projected in the original plan.

▸ Secured a bylined article for Ashen in *Hotel Business Review.*

▸ Conducted an extensive audit with dash design's clients and associates to see how the company was perceived by those it does business with (revisit Tip #2, back in Chapter 1). The nine-page summary report helped identify existing strengths, as well as areas that needed to be focused on in the public relations plan and outreach efforts.

▸ Produced a media list featuring more than 1,500 print, broadcast, and online press outlets as well as a comprehensive editorial calendar of upcoming story opportunities in national and global trade and consumer outlets.

▸ Produced a social media memorandum with recommendations on leveraging LinkedIn and Facebook, suggestions on which groups to join, guidance on how senior executives could be more active on the company page, and a proposal for better engaging audiences to increase firm visibility. We also produced nearly three dozen items for the client to post.

‣ Secured a spot for Ashen at the highly coveted Hotel Business Design Executive Roundtable, a key industry trade venue. An editorial placement will occur. Hence, two objectives—a speaking engagement and media—were achieved.

‣ Enriched the program with select off-program tactics—including an introduction to a senior-level executive at a major hotel chain—that added value at no additional cost to the client.

‣ ‣ ‣

And with that, fellow entrepreneur, we have come to the conclusion of *The Little Book of Big PR.* I hope you found this guidance helpful. These tips and case studies are based on my thirty-plus years in the industry as well as real-world experience. All of my tips have been successfully employed, in one form or the other, by my clients—and me! Now go out there and get your "unfair share" of attention!

ENDNOTES

CHAPTER 1

1. Tom Peters, *Fast Company*, "The Brand Called You" (New York: Mansueto Ventures, LLC, August/September, 1997); www.fastcompany.com/28905/brand-called-you.

2. Wikipedia, www.en.wikipedia.org/wiki/Personal_branding.

3. Peters, *Fast Company*, 1997.

CHAPTER 3

1. Lori Ruff, *KISSmetrics,* blog written by Jesse Aaron of WebpageFX; blog.kissmetrics.com/50-social-media-influencers/.

2. The Nielsen Company, "State of the Media: The Social Media Report of 2012" (New York and Diemen, the Netherlands: Nielsen Holdings N.V., 2012), p. 2; www.nielsen.com/us/en/reports/2012/state-of-the-media-the-social-media-report-2012.html/.

CHAPTER 4

1. Armstrong Williams, www.brainyquote.com/quotes/quotes/a/armstrongw291564.html/.

CHAPTER 5

1. Michelle Mazur, "5 of the Smartest Things Ever Said About Public Speaking" (YAHOO! Small Business Advisor, 2013); https://smallbusiness.yahoo.com/advisor/5-smartest-things-ever-said-public-speaking-213015246.html.

2. "Fear of Public Speaking Statistics," Statistic Brain (2012 Statistic Brain Research publishing as Statistic Brain, 2012); www.statisticbrain.com/fear-of-public-speaking-statistics.

CHAPTER 6

1. The Nielsen Company, "Consumers Who Care and Say They'll Reward Companies with Their Wallets" (New York and Diemen, the Netherlands: Nielsen Holdings N.V., August 2013), p. 4; www.nielsen.com/content/dam/corporate/us/en/reports-downloads/2013%20Reports/Nielsen-Global-Report-Consumers-Who-Care-August-2013.pdf.

CHAPTER 7

1. Bill Gates, *The Content Factory*, Online PR, Social Media Marketing & Web Content Writing (2013); www.contentfac.com/damn-i-wish-id-said-that-50-of-our-favorite-pr-quotes/.

INDEX

ABOUT THE AUTHOR

Jennefer Witter is the CEO and founder of The Boreland Group Inc. (TBG), a boutique public relations agency headquartered in New York City with a presence in the Washington, D.C., metropolitan area. Certified as a woman-owned business, TBG was recognized by TheStreet.com in 2012 as one of five black-owned businesses in the country "making a buzz." Jennefer was ranked as one of the top ten black CEOs and entrepreneurs in the nation by *MadameNoire* magazine in 2013.

Jennefer is a thirty-plus-year PR veteran. She has been quoted in many leading media outlets, including the Associated Press, TheStreet.com, MarketWatch Radio Network, and *Crain's New York Business* on public relations, small business, and social media subjects. She has presented on numerous public relations topics at venues such as The Communication Leadership Exchange 2014 Annual Conference, Ellevate (formerly 85 Broads), GlobalWIN, The Power Conference, New York University, and The Science, Industry and Business Library.

Jennefer was formerly the Inc.com TV PR expert and was a contributor to AOL Small Business. Prior to starting TBG in 2003, she was a vice president at Ketchum, a global public relations firm.

Jennefer received her Bachelor of Arts degree in Communications (Print Journalism) from Fordham University, and considers herself a lifelong learner.

Learn more about Jennefer's company and her accomplishments on her website at www.theborelandgroup.com, or contact her directly at LittleBookofBigPR@theborelandgroup.com.

CPSIA information can be obtained at www.ICGtesting.com
Printed in the USA
BVOW08s2157150715

409051BV00004B/52/P